ANCHOR
BOOKS

A POETIC FORMULA

Edited by

Simon Harwin

First published in Great Britain in 2003 by
ANCHOR BOOKS
Remus House,
Coltsfoot Drive,
Peterborough, PE2 9JX
Telephone (01733) 898102

SB ISBN 1 84418 245 2

FOREWORD

Anchor Books is a small press, established in 1992, with the aim of promoting readable poetry to as wide an audience as possible.

We hope to establish an outlet for writers of poetry who may have struggled to see their work in print.

The poems presented here have been selected from many entries, and as always editing proved to be a difficult task.

I trust this selection will delight and please the authors and all those who enjoy reading poetry.

Simon Harwin
Editor

CONTENTS

THE FOX

As down the country lane I passed
A fox a wary eye on me cast
I told him just get out of here
The hounds and huntsmen are very near.
I can hear horns and the baying of hounds
Don't you think you are out of bounds?
The look he gave was one of despair
It seemed to say does anyone care?
Go to the river and try to hide
Run across to the other side
When they come as I'm sure they will
A fugitive they'll not be able to kill.
Then hoofbeats approached with a terrible din
He flashed his brush and seemed to grin
Away he sped to the water's side
And although they hunted far and wide
The fox lived on till another time
And that is the reason for my rhyme.

M Sanderson

THE BALLAD OF GREY RIVER BEND

Ride to the call of the wind, my friend,
Ride to the chill of its voice,
For there's only one end
And there ain't no real choice
When you meet at the Grey River Bend.

A man's waiting there with his back to the light,
They know him as Poker Sharp Sam,
He's a face like the night
And he don't give a damn
In his reckoning of who figures right.

You crossed him last Fall in the town of Snake Sands,
Played high to his stakes in the game,
But gave him no edge to his fancy demands,
Not a hint or the spit of a name
As he slid that marked card through his hands.

Sam drew with a snarl at the mention of 'Cheat',
With a look of cold death in his eye.
'I'll see you in Hell, there is no retreat,
And I'll ask you to swallow that lie,
Or spell out the place and a time when we meet.'

Sleep was no peace as you waited for dawn
And the climb of the sun to your fate,
You sweated to hear the laughter and scorn,
The sneers in that gunslinger's hate,
But vowed he'd regret the sad day he was born.

So ride to the call of the wind, my old friend,
And the chill of its echoing voice,
For it's told of the end
On the last breath of choice,
In the showdown at Grey River Bend.

Brian Parvin

BALLAD FOR A PRESIDENT, 2003

The President of the USA,
Anticipating a happy day,
Surveys the crowd and tries,
With lazy smile and half-shut eyes,
To savour his increasing power
Able to beguile folk by the hour
With rousing words of raw emotion,
His special form of a magic potion.

War's the theme and war's the aim,
Ensuring him some hollow fame.
Brutality replaces sanity,
Legality and all humanity.
First Iraq, then Syria next
There's always some false, fake pretext.
He feels safe, power-drunk and fine,
Confidently ignorant, right on line.

With an English prime minister,
In a way vaguely sinister,
Following this dangerous fool
Acting as his worldwide tool
To help destroy lives, hope and culture,
Denying us any shred of a future.
The President savours his call to war
What alternative has he to go for?

S J Dodwell

MISMATCH

Of a single prince a king did heed;
a very suitable catch indeed,
he considered for his daughter fair,
most musical suitor anywhere
as classical excerpts sweet princess
produced with ardent, royal finesse
on the harp, the cello, violin,
and so many wished her heart to win;
the emperors' sons of countless realms;
said King, 'The thought of it overwhelms,
but ear for music takes pride of place,
whatever creed the couple embrace.'
The king alike was symphony mad,
wrote to Prince Rex and said he'd be glad
if he his musical child might meet
but, alas, these strivings met defeat;
Rex arrived but was given the boot -
'Father, that interloper won't suit,'
said she, 'one man band? It's got to stop!
My idea of music *is not* pop!'
With strings of her harp resided pluck
her dad and Prince Rex were out of luck.

Ruth Daviat

THE HOME BUILDERS
(Viewed from a kitchen window)

In spring two blackbirds, cock and mate,
A family did contemplate.
Said she, 'My love I cannot rest
Till we have found a place to nest.
It must be snug and off the ground
So where can such a place be found?'
Now at the garden's farthest edge
There grew a dense and prickly hedge,
Good cover from frost, rain or snow,
Secure from hunting cats below.
Said he, 'My dear, now am I right
To think that just the perfect site,
Where you and I could raise our chicks
Quite safe from weather's wildest tricks?'
The two set out that very hour
The verges all around to scour
For moss and roots and grass and straw,
Amassing quite a goodly store.
In truth they scarcely stopped to feed
Until they had supplied their need.
A sparrow in the honeysuckle
Watched and gave a wily chuckle.
He too had a nest to build.
A roguish thought his mind had filled.
He flew across to take a peek,
Emerged grass dangling from his beak.
Oh you lazy, thieving bird!
For shame! Now have you never heard
That stealing is a wicked crime?
Go forage for yourself next time.

V E Godfrey

REPLACING THE 'P' WITH A 'G'

From the depths of despair, I eventually found me,
behind all the pain I could never just be.
Those thoughts and feelings I used to dread,
but as I did before, I never said.

The doors were locked; I'd misplaced the key,
although without it, I knew I'd never see.
There was much beyond that door,
but I ignored the pain, never getting to the core.

To hide away and not to care,
it was that I couldn't bear.
I needed direction for me to live,
without the courage there was no give.

You see what you want to see,
be what you want to be.
Then, the dilemma of life,
with its twists and turns it cuts like a knife.

The choice is always there;
at times it just doesn't seem fair.
Then light appears at the road with no end,
the thought diminished that you're round the bend.

Looking back to the past is not living;
it's receiving and learning all that life is giving.
Learn to live through the confusion and the pain;
it's the only way through life you stand to gain.

Nicola Goodison

THE CLOSING SONG

What chance of the gentle rain refreshing
by small drops caressing an upturned face
when there is nothing to receive a blessing
like neglected garden of a former place
no help to a life for growing on
the will to be revived already gone.
    Eagerly he came to write new songs
    an absent father's old guitar to play
    having left that house of many wrongs
    to alternative and better living anyway
    brilliant an edge to helping tunes along
    under stars to sleep, and feeling strong.
Becoming busking partner to a team
promising to take all on and far
but that move became a shattered dream
the others waking early, taking the guitar
a valued present to a father's son
everything was missing; all the money gone.
    Hard hitting the result for all he shared
    sharp in loneliness with no one else around
    a broken trust when he thought they cared
    only the result of loss was to be found
    not success within his make-shift home
    then falling down as heavy as a stone.
Life had washed away to falling rain
hope flattened in composer and musician
the others yet to realise only minimum of gain
as the best of songs remained unwritten
although his effort made, should not be forgotten
now potential in misfortune to someone else's song.

Reg C H Baggs

THE WORLD ROLLS BY

Birds are flying in the sky
As I just watch the world roll by
And stars twinkle oh so bright
As they light up the night
But then come the dawn
And all my dreams are gone
Dogs still run down the lane
Oh how I wish I could see you again
Sometimes I just wonder why
You left without even saying goodbye
As I start another day
I wonder if you will pass my way
And if you did would you stop and talk
Or just carry on and walk
And all day long I long for it to be night
When once again I will have you in my sight
So now the world just rolls on by
And I am left alone to cry
I know there is no one to blame
But it really is a shame.

Eileen Kyte

DRIFTING

Pods of cloud drift slowly by,
Floating on an endless sigh,
High above the thoughts of man
Billowing gypsies caravan.

Beneath their drift, green machines,
Turning soil in silver seams,
The combing out of nature's hair,
Preparing for her season's dare.

A timid whistle faintly sings
Of memories wove from former things,
A steam train pushing through the heath,
A line of breath its fading wreath.

From the wires crows magistrate
With rook and jay in harsh debate
While lapwings loop their lover's dance,
Spurred by spring and Cupid's lance.

A crowded world to look upon,
Yet lonely when your love has gone,
And all that's left to do is sigh,
As pods of cloud drift slowly by.

Tony Cullen

MOURNING GRACE

It is with sadness he does roam,
Along the seashore watching the foam,
The cruel sea that stole his wife,
How can he steer through his life.
Gone is she that bore him child,
Carefree children left to run wild,
Grief and anger eat him up inside.
For the brutal murderess cannot hide,
Biding time for the souls, she sleeps.
Salty tears run down his face,
Sweet memories of his love Grace,
Only eight short years of marriage,
What's left of life for him to salvage?
Around his feet the children play,
Too young to know she's gone away.
With broken heart he kneels to God,
Why forsake a mother so good?
Keep her heart mine for evermore,
While I kneel mourning by the shore.

Jane Margaret Isaac

MY FANTASTIC PRESENT

As I was homebound on the train
Above me flew that fantastic plane
A plane on which I once flew
With my late love, just we two.
For my fiftieth birthday such a surprise
A dream come true, brought tears to my eyes
A day out in Paris under April's sun
Then a flight back on Concorde. Number one!
Beautiful Paris with my beautiful wife
Lunch alfresco by the Seine. What a life!
Then at Charles de Gaulle airport the sleek bird
Just waiting for us, asleep, unheard
The power of take off, through sound barrier to mach two
With laughter and dinner, champagne too.
Now my love's in paradise, cut down in her prime
Carried away at just forty-nine
No fiftieth celebrations to enjoy with her
Which makes her present mean so much more
And Concorde's being retired never again to fly
Nothing to replace her presence in the sky
Great memories as I read my certificate, framed
Wonderful day, wonderful girl, and wonderful plane.

Mike Jackson

SOMETHING AMISS

Mine introspective feckless brain
Gyrates forlorn o'er'n empty plain,
Revealed in countryside so bland,
Whereon, I own, to stare and stand.
I cast me back with tears that sting,
An owl's hoot-hoot re-echoing,
Whence underneath, the brushwood stirs -
Among the hillside's conifers.
A badger stops, and peers, and snorts -
And sifts the leafmould as it sorts
Fain unaware of company,
Within a silent sanctuary.
Bright moonlight, atmospheric, shines,
As all the family now dines,
For one by one, without a sound,
They've now appeared from out the ground -
To chunter on their well-worn beat,
For something wonderful to eat.
Many-a-night I've sat entranced -
E'erlong my heart in ardour danced.
Many-a-moon of yore hath shone.
Many-a-moment's come and gone.
Many-a-time I've rued the day -
They took the badgers all away.

D Haskett-Jones

THE FATE OF BRAVE MARCUS

As Marcus rows his boat away
On moonlit waters shadows play,
A spray of mystery all around
The air is silent, not a sound.

An air of danger, darkness falls
A voice that moans and wails and calls,
And dreary waters of deep gloom
A warning of forthcoming doom.

The mainland now has gone from sight
As Marcus now resolves to fight.
A creature who disturbs each hour
Creating mystery with such power.

His body trembles with great fear
To face the cause, the time is near,
Deserted island, none to heed
No witness can record this deed.

The boat now dragged onto the beach
There lies a monster, out of reach,
He rears up high, then jaws close tight,
The empty boat drifts out of sight.

Irene Grahame

SIR GODFREY AND THE DRAGON

Godfrey lived in days of old,
Of all knights he was most bold,
But one thing was very plain
His great fault was he was vain.

Pinned up on a forest tree,
So that passers-by could see,
A notice caught Sir Godfrey's eye
(This is something I must try.)
In the town of Forest Way
A dragon has come down today,
Stolen Princess Phylador,
Threatens to abduct some more.
And the one who puts to sword
This dragon, earns a great reward.

Late that night Sir Godfrey rose,
In the square he struck a pose.
'Come on, dragon, meet me here.
I'm the one you have to fear.'
The dragon gave a mighty roar,
Lashed Sir Godfrey to the floor,
But his tail caught on the sword
Of the boastful, fallen lord.
In a flash the knight struck out.
Of his skill there was no doubt.

On the ground the dragon lay
Minus tail - he'd lost the day.
Godfrey gained his just reward,
Thanks to his triumphant sword.

Stephanie Stone

MABEL

Her father was a sailor, mother had been a cook,
Mabel worked for a tailor and liked to read a book.
Mabel was now twenty and since she was seven
She'd wanted money, plenty, riches were her heaven.
Of handsome prince she dreamed, he was her spouse to be.
Mabel sewed and schemed, an optimist was she.
'You're wasting all your time,' said Mother, 'reading lies.'
She said, 'It is no crime, and authors, they are wise.'
'Why not find a nice boy, an honest working man?
It's to a woman's joy to marry if she can.
He may be a sailor, a soldier or a cook,
Or you may find a tailor, but not inside a book.'
Mabel was now thirty and still she worked and schemed.
Some men were very flirty, but of her prince she dreamed.
Mabel was quite pretty, attractive figure too.
To men it seemed a pity she did not want to woo.
Our Mabel sat and sewed and Mother shook her head.
'When you're an ugly toad you'll wish that you were dead.'
Mabel was now forty and was attractive still.
Her suitors found her haughty, she would not say 'I will'
They told her she was missing all good things in life,
The cuddling and the kissing, she'd make a charming wife.
Mabel was now fifty - her beauty, it had waned.
Although she was still thrifty her poverty remained.
Her father and her mother, both of them had died.
No sister or a brother, in loneliness she cried.
Couples in the street - how happy they did look!
She had no man to greet, companion was a book.
They found her in the river. Nobody really cared.
Perhaps she'd a bad liver, and took her life while scared.

F G Ward

THE BALLAD OF QUINTON HOUSE

Quinton House lay in the valley of Rosebud Vale
A valley so beautiful, one can never fail
To see so divine beauty and the house
Was pink glazed stone, double fronted with a joust
Yard behind where friends enjoyed
The sport so immensely they toyed
With the idea of blending fun and games
Together at every season of the year
James Quinton, was a man full of vim and vigour
He was so full of life, a gold digger
When a friend had a dilemma, he would use his ploy trigger
Slapping him on the back with a powerful right hand
'Come on dear fellow,' he would bellow, 'lend
My friend; to others, all your support.' They knew better
Than to refuse, he had his way to the letter
There came a day when things went wrong
James Quinton was now not so strong
His days in India when a youth
Caught up with him and so now lay in bed in the south
Wing of Quinton House, sadly stricken by malaria
His fair-weather friends soon fortook his area
Poor James Quinton recovered but weak with the disease
Quinton House still stood blooming in the midday sun
In the beautiful valley of Rosebud Vale, the fun
Of the joust yard still echoing of the horses run
James Quinton's new friends were so very different
Kind, loving, dependable, desirable and decent.

Alma Montgomery Frank

WHAT IS A POEM?

Does a poem have to rhyme?
If so, it takes time,
Time needs motion,
Motion has a study,
Study brings a group,
A group becomes a troupe,
A troupe needs a colour,
Colour prevents pallor,
Pallor becomes iller,
Iller brings death -
Death prevents breath.
Breath gives life,
Life causes strife,
Strife turns to worry,
Worry makes you hurry,
Hurry is a rush -
Rush to the flush,
Flush in the face,
Face shows the race,
Race takes the pace,
Pace shows your speed -
Speed gathers time,
Time causes rhythm,
Rhythm turns to rhyme,
Rhyme is the reason,
The reason is rhyme.

Pat Derbyshire

FLOREAT SALOPIA

Down a long and winding rural road
High hedges either side,
Revealing secrets, oh so slow!
Heart's ease at end of ride.

Five good roses round my door
Sup for the honey bee,
My Lord shall know me even more
In such tranquillity.

I do not need a castle home
Nor yet a manor fair,
A little cot so I don't roam,
But love must linger there.

A little cot of simple mein
But weatherproof withal,
A place that's heard the Ancients sing
Seen kingdoms rise and fall.

That's stood against the weather's force
That's faced both frost and hail,
That knows the growing pains of spring
That summer's sometimes fail.

Two great trees about my cot
For shield and summer shade,
The oak for shield that seldom rots
The last of leaves to fade.

The aspen for the sound of waves
Breaking on the shore,
The wind will write those music staves
And I'll not want for more.

About my cot, there'll be a plot
Where sheep may safely graze,
And at their call, I will recall
And change my foolish ways.

Do not grieve when I am lost
Beat no path to door,
My words like empty husks are tossed
Far from the winnowing floor.

No soft-shoed Pantaloon shall shout
'Arrest!' at poet's grave,
The Ship of Fools shall go about
A poet's soul to save.

Graham K A Walker

FLAME

A wick flairs then burns.
Candlelight now bright reveals
A room once concealed.

John Pegg

THE WAY AHEAD

The way ahead is clearly marked
Heights and lows, pubs and steeples
Highlit roads blazed through roundabouts
Lefts and rights, rivers crossed

Heights and lows, pubs and steeples
Signposts help the ebb and flow
Lefts and rights, rivers crossed
Destination to my loves in good time

Signposts help the ebb and flow
Highlit roads blazed through roundabouts
Destination to my loves in good time
The way ahead was clearly marked.

Michael Alan Fenton

MISSILES

Unearthly light over the city . . .
An explosion rips the night apart
Strategic site or palace hit?
Empty or crowded market square?

An explosion rips the night apart
Oncoming missile - where will it strike?
Strategic site or palaces hit?
The guilty or the innocent?

Oncoming missile - where will it strike?
Strategic site or palace hit?
The guilty or the innocent?
Unearthly light over the city . . .

Chris Creedon

REMAINS

1	2
Leaves	Litter

Dropped -	Dropped -
by hands	by little
of city trees	city hands *passing through*
will be gone	will remain

Dropped -	Remain -
between paving,	until the leaves
roads,	are gone
car parks,	
drives	Until -
	I,
Gone -	you, we
before the sun	are gone
crumbles	
the summer soil	Until -
	our roots are gone
Ready -	
to re-give	Until -
themselves to	the hands themselves
their roots	have dropped
again	*or passed through*

Lorenzo Quanla

THERE WAS AN...

There was an old git called Devine
Who swallowed a bottle of wine,
Along with his will,
And a foul-tasting pill,
And so Devine died 'intestine'.

Robert Kennedy

UNTITLED

A working man who bore the name of Toodles
Was eating HP Sauce with buttered noodles,
As he chewed a slippery bite
He thought, it isn't right
To give my name to Pomeranians and poodles.

Kathleen Goodwin

AN ANTI-SOCIAL RABBIT

There once was a very large rabbit
who, on seeing an apple would grab it.
His brow then would furrow,
for those in the burrow
thought this was a very bad habit.

K Newbrook

LAMENT

'A limerick's *so* drefful diffy -
I thought I'd write one in a jiffy!'
Cried Georgie, in pain,
'Though I've tried, might and main,
The result is quite frightfully iffy.'

Patricia Fallace

TO AN ANEMONE

Wraith of the long winter night,
Essence of spring Immortelle!
Miracle graven in white,
Pale little mademoiselle -,
Sailing your green caravel,
Why is your rigging so sleek?
Whence your immaculate gel?
Woodland anemone speak!

Wings you upraise to the night,
Fabergé eye in a shell,
Slender chemise for a sprite,
Laved by the moon in the dell -
Daylight and dawn will dispel
Tears that dishevelled your cheek,
Teach me your secret, oh tell!
Woodland anemone speak!

Zephyrs of spring you delight,
Fondly your pinions outswell,
Panting with curtsy polite,
Pirouette little gay Asphodel!
Frail petit fey bagatelle,
Tinged with that purplish streak,
Smiling your magical spell,
Woodland anemone speak!

Envoy

Here where in dapples you dwell,
Breezes betremble your cheek,
Was it from Heaven you fell?
Woodland anemone speak!

Terence Belford

LUNCHTIME BITE

As I work now at this ballad
Eating my sandwich with salad,
The bright sun is out and it's hot,
But chill in the wind when it's not.
The ham's tender and not too thin
And the toms are minus their skin,
Spring onions are cut to a ring
And watercress makes it all sing.
There's butter not marg in-between
Quite all right, yet seldom seen;
The bread's cut thin, medium or thick,
Brown and white, so I take my pick.
The chap's grub, near me's, in a box
With cheese; reminiscent of socks;
I don't mind sardines from a tin,
Though prawns in sauce don't make you thin!
I've now eaten mine; so what's next?
If I drop crumbs, folks'll be vexed,
But we lads enjoy outdoor fare,
And lasses' smiles 'neath blossom'd hair.

Dennis Marshall

LIMERICK

There was a young lady from Ware
With beautiful raven black hair
She had such a fright
It went white overnight
And now she's a freak at the fair.

Neil Dewhurst

DEAD FOX ON THE HIGHWAY

Vulpes Alepex, born of elegance and grace
Your beauty has passed into death
I gaze upon your reddish-brown fur lined face
As I catch my sharpened breath.

Your beauty has passed into death
On this urban road in the early morning
As I catch my sharpened breath
I pray your cubs heed this fatal warning.

On this urban road in the early morning
I gaze upon your reddish-brown fur lined face
I pray your cubs heed this fatal warning
Vulpes Alepex, born of elegance and grace.

Keith Tissington

CRIME OF PASSION

'Twas early in the morning mist,
The girl I loved, she was being kissed
By the dearest friend I thought I did have,
But no longer is he, for he's dead in his grave.
How it did happen, I'll never know,
For my senses had left me, and a rage it did grow.
She was saying, 'Kiss me, not once but twice,
For your kisses are tingling my bones and it's nice.'
He smiled and his hand caressed her sweet face,
And she lifted her head and her finger did trace,
Round the shape of his lips, then her hand round his neck,
And she pulled him towards her, 'twas then I felt sick.
I leapt in-between them, my knife in my hand,
Then blank went my mind. Though you'll ne'er understand
The reason the memory's so blurred and unreal,
Is until you have suffered the pain and ordeal.
I'll be found guilty of murder intent,
But I assure you it wasn't, for my mind it was bent.
And now I'll be gone to find me a tree,
From which I shall hang for my lover to see.

Monica D Buxton

To A Daisy

Gold sunbeam in a ballet skirt, swan-white
From ribbons, ofttimes tipped with ruby, made,
Born but to bless, thou bloom'st in beauty bright,
Starring the grassy common, verge and glade;
And in the ancient churchyard, o'er the sleep
Of those who wreathless and forgotten lie,
Eternal, loving vigil thou dost keep,
With tear of dewdrop glist'ning in thine eye;
Deemed insignificant, oft called a weed,
Yet those who take the time to study thee,
Find thou art wonderfully wrought, indeed,
With childlike charm and gracious symmetry;
Dear Heav'n! The world would be a lesser place,
Without thy joyous little upturned face.

Muriel Willa

WHITE HORSE HILL

To walk on White Horse Hill alone at dawn,
yet not alone, for let the silence sing
the secrets of the smithy's ancient stone,
of Beakers and of Blowing Stone and King:
a fortress here on White Horse Hill stands guard
near Dragon hill the manger of a god,
an ancient myth, his horse was ridden hard
to Waylands where the smith his steed once shod.
Now is one's conscious mind content to rest,
the spirit's mind waits on the hill to hear
the orchestra of silence at its best,
sound wordless sonnets of the timeless seer:
in fragile form a skylark flies its nest,
sings of that love by all true life confessed.

Peter Fahy

IN LOVING MEMORY
(Sonnet in memory of a lost love)

I called her my dear lovely darling when
I wrote to her; and when I rang each day
I never missed the opportunity to say
How much I loved her. Time and time again
I hit on ways of rushing to her side,
And down the years drove many thousand miles
To hold her in my arms and see her smiles
Of pleasure as she welcomed me inside
Her safe, warm home. But though those magic days
Are long since gone, when stressed I need her still,
And constantly repeated in the restless mill
Of my sad mind I hear the urgent phrase:
'I want to go to Marjorie' as though
She's waiting there: alas, she's not, I know.

Frank Littlewood

THE EPISTLE

Do you remember, all those years ago?

How,

We dipped through orchard valleys,
laced with morning ghosts,
angel corkscrews, twisting heavenward.

We rattled rhythmical past trees,
rich, and hung heavy with images of the sun -
plump, golden spheres,
pink-tinged with sunrise.

We sat on wall of burning stone,
at midday,
in Po Valley's oven -
sinking teeth into welcome juice,
taking bites from sun-like orbs,
as an eclipsing moon.

We woke, in cloistered peace,
to holy chorus -
dark angels in earthly paradise.

We looked and saw the bloom
from angels' cheeks,
and dew, like tears,
on those same heaven-fruits,
in sacred square of green.

We saw them, piled in pyramid of pure colour,
climbing to salute the virgin,
on her marble plinth -
catching shafts of filtered gold-dust,
through windows of the outer world,
and settling in pools of faith.

But, enough of peaches!
We swam in tepid, midnight sea,
and laughed in Luna Park.

Under a slice of moon,
like honeyed melon.

Jennifer D Wootton

UNTITLED

A rose lover whose blooms drooped pathetically,
Assumed they'd grown rather too energetically.
But a rose bush that grows
The same length as a hose,
Has to have been, engineered, genetically.

M Roach

THE QUESTION I HATE

Why do people all want money?
Whether used for good or greed,
They say that it's as sweet as honey,
And everyone seems to follow the lead.

Whether used for good or greed,
People always seem to want more money,
And everyone seems to follow the lead,
Whether the weather is rainy or sunny.

People always seem to want more money,
For their own material wealth,
Whether the weather is rainy or sunny,
It's beginning to affect our health.

For their own material wealth,
Whether they're corrupt or great,
It's beginning to affect our health,
And it gives the question that I hate.

Whether they're corrupt or great,
They say that it's as sweet as honey,
And it gives the question that I hate,
Why do people all want money?

Oliver Butler (14)

THE SNAKE

The snake slides through the grass
Its green coils flowing
Moving swiftly
With eyes, two green slits

Its green coils flowing
A mere rustle in the brown
With eyes, two green slits
It looks

A mere rustle in the brown
The sun baking its scales
It looks
Forked tongue hissing in apprehension

The sun baking its scales
The blue sky, parchment dry
Forked tongue hissing in apprehension
It finally sights prey

The blue sky, parchment dry
Moving swiftly
It finally sights prey
The snake slides through the grass

Charis Bredin (13)

LIMERICK

A worshipping lady of Crewe
To church took her pet cockatoo.
When the minister read
The cockatoo said:
'Turn to hymn number 72.'

Ivan S Thomas

UNTITLED

There was an old woman from Looe
For dinner each day she ate stew
The meat was 'pindy', which made her quite 'windy'
The folk in her street all said, 'Phew!'

G D Furse

DR FROM GLOUCESTER

An old man from Gloucester, named Cain,
A medical man, quite insane,
Stepped into a puddle,
And got in a muddle,
Whenever he saw folks in pain.

Joyce Walker

LIMERICK

There once was a boy from Jersey
Who dreamed of swimming the River Mersey
To Liverpool he came
But his memory went lame
So he went back home to live on Guernsey!

Colin Jones

HYPOCHONDRIAC

I swallow all the pills and potions,
No cure-all do I lack,
My friends think I'm crazy,
But I'm a hypochondriac -
I'm afraid to get any disease,
Because I always think it must be fatal,
When I get a cough or sneeze.
I've got cures for things,
Like rabies, cholera and gout.
I hope I never catch them,
But I don't want to be caught out.
I always wear a face mask,
So that I cannot get into trouble.
My home is a germ-free bubble,
If all my precautions do not work,
Then the only solution that is left.
I will not go out at all,
So that the bugs can't get me,
In that case, I might probably
Starve to death.

F C Pelton

WITH CREAM?

There was a clever old auk
Who learned how to eat with a fork
As he flew through the sky
With a plate of fruit pie
There was often a great deal of talk

Joan Briggs

THE PRICE OF LOVE

She waited long for his approach,
No more for her the family coach,
Bareback on a tired mare,
Passers-by did stop to stare.
For their glances cared she not,
In Cupid's web of love, now caught,
With handsome, dark-eyed, lusty lover,
Her eyes of blue can see no other.
Banished from her childhood homestead,
Discovering love - within his bed.
He comes, she mounts, escape tonight,
Soon they disappear from sight,
Her maidenhead will sure be lost,
Foolish girl, you'll count the cost.
Life of hardship, hunger, toil,
Spent in tilling Adam's soil.
Oh feckless maid of seventeen,
A drudge, instead of England's queen.

Pamela Carder

SPOOKS

The watchers that watch are never seen
The intruder not there and has not been
That perfumed smell that's in the air
Is not the proof of anyone there
The ear piece of the listeners' trade
A wire to hear, not to evade
You will not hear the tap on the phone
But it will click when you are not home
A shadow moves just out of cinque
Tricks the light, a mind's eye blink
That ornament that is out of place
Can be your sanity, saving grace
Are you sure what you did that day?
Will you disapprove what they all say?
You may be watched and your phone tapped
Whilst into a jacket you are strapped
The facts will fit if ever they can
You are their target and so their man
While watching watchers remain unseen
The secret police have never been.

J P Worthy

PETE

There was a young boy called Pete,
Whose mum said he had to be neat.
So he cleaned his room,
But came to his doom,
When his mum said she could still smell his feet!

N Cobham

EXPERIMENT

The ancients had a word for them, the men from 'out of space',
Forbears, ancestors, what you will, who put us in this place!
They seeded us and left us to do the best we can,
And we have gone on living to carry out their plan.

Do they watch us down the years, their big experiment?
Do they wonder at our fears and our search for what is meant
By our lives as we live them, the ills that beset us too?
If we have left the petri dish, what will our sponsors do?

Will they rub us out without a care, like swatting a fly
Or will they keep a careful watch as centuries go by?
They tried the giant lizards once, encouraged them to breed,
To fill the Earth with varied life - this was their first 'seed'!

The dinosaurs upset them, we don't know in what way,
So they rubbed them out completely, and then they tried again!
Man and all his artefacts they planted long ago.
They'll check up when they pass this way, as round the spheres they go!

> How shall we measure up?
> And if we don't, what then?
> Who can guess what their standards are?
> These 'more than', 'less than' men!

Joyce M Jones

NUMBER TEN

I'd hate to live in number ten
To please all people, how or when
Now ask yourself, what would you do
To equalise all people too?

Some want this, and others that
Pompous words so matter of fact
It can't be easy when you rule
To deal with jesters playing the fool.

Whoever lives at number ten
There isn't one to please all men
So many cynics in every race
Lots would like to take his place.

I envy not; his high position
To go to war! What a decision
Everybody is wanting more
Opposition do hold the floor.

This Earth, this land will always be
Ruled by people with faults like me
Let us all try to be friends
Until we reach the final end.

Joan Prentice

MY SPECIAL PLACES

I love the Channel Islands so
The sea of azure blue enchants me
At every opportunity I must go

Those puffins on the rugged rocks
A sight of beauty and nature free
I love the Channel Islands so

Jersey's beautiful, cows so brown
And the pretty Jersey lily for all to see
At every opportunity I must go

Alderney's lighthouse with its flashing dome
Island hospitality is the best there can be
I love the Channel Islands so

Guernsey with flowers grown on its cliffs
That dramatically sweep down to the sea
At every opportunity I must go

These enchanting isles I've come to know
They're like a second home to me
I love the Channel Islands so
At every opportunity I must go.

Anthony Gibson

THIS MOMENT IN TIME

Everything seems to be
Planned as we grow
How soon the years fly
To where, nobody knows
There is so much to do
In this moment in time
You look back, reflect
Was this all really mine?
This life that I lived
Has brought so much and more
Where love is forever
Just there at the door
Rewarding and happy
My halcyon days
Now peaceful as ever
While I travel life's way
I wouldn't change anything
Life's taught me much
For as I've learned gladly
Then so I have taught

Jeanette Gaffney

I KNOW YOU

I've seen you around.
I know your face so well.
And if you were to look at me
I think you'd hear the bell.
But I don't know how to reach you,
or how to make you mine.
And I think my days are numbered
'cause I'm running out of time.
But I've been so very close to you,
with no distance in between.
You have been my king
while I have been your queen.
I wonder if you know it too,
if you're searching for my face,
but don't know how to find me
outside the dreaming place.
So I'll see you when I sleep love,
and I'll keep looking for a way,
to take you from my slumber,
and make you real someday.

M M Graham

ALIVE

Poetry in motion, like a bird upon the wing,
Heavenly music, to hear the blackbird sing.
Buttercups and daisies, daffodils dancing in the breeze,
Greenery in hedgerows, blossoms weigh down trees.
Perfume of roses, lilac and sweet peas,
Puffins and seagulls, as they dive to the seas.
Colours of nature, butterfly wings,
Peacocks, flamingos, such beautiful things.
Chicks in the farmyard, lambs in green field,
The wonder of nature in lifestyle revealed.

E M Gough

OH DEAR! OH DEAR!

Oh dear! Oh dear! Such a beautiful thing.
I've never seen a thrush up close, only heard one sing.
It just seemed to land on my van.
I'm powerless to help it, I need someone who can.
It's bleeding so much from its broken wing.

Its left leg just seems to be dangling.
Have you got a vet's number I can ring?
This day seemed like any other when it began.
Oh dear! Oh dear!

Who knows what each day will bring?
Things just have a habit of happening.
They don't seem to be controlled by man.
Who'd want to include death in their plan?
At least now it's dead, it's not suffering.
Oh dear! Oh dear!

Rosina L Gutcher

THANK YOU FRIENDS AND FAMILY

So many people have sped through my life,
I'd need every page in a book -
To name them and thank them for just 'being there'
Apart from the trouble they took -
- To call at my home with some flowers or a smile
To brighten the days that are sad,
They all play a part, wiping tears from the heart,
Growing old is not nearly so bad.

Monica C Gibson

THANK YOU

I express myself with gratitude,
Of all you have helped me through.
Encouraged me as a fighter,
And made me believe in me like you do.

I appreciate your helping hand,
When I needed it so.
You put me back into line,
And I am grateful, you helped me internally grow.

I *thank you* for what I am now,
Because I would have never been like this,
Without your support and willingness,
I am now living in Heaven and bliss.

You must be more than a friend,
Because you have always apprehended.
You are always there for me,
Until the very end.

Once again, I am so thankful,
And dedicate this to you,
For I can not return any favours,
That compare to the same favours you have done for me
                                                    all year through.

I hope you accept my thank you poem, please, I hope you do,
Reciprocation, my life, I owe to you.

Angela Tsang

Rondeau For A Fender Stratocaster Guitar

A red Fender strat was the dream of us all,
If we played The Palladium, or Grays Co-Op hall,
A guitar like 'The Shads' used was really the tops,
If your group had ambitions for 'Top Of The Pops',
The only guitar that could rise to the call.

The sounds you could get were the greatest of all,
There was nothing to touch the deep twang and the thrall of
A red Fender.

It's still the guitar that is better than all
Rickenbackers and Gibsons, there's none can forestall
A red Fender.

Mick Nash

WHEELY-BIN VITAMINS

The diet's never changed. It is the same
each day, each week - down every street you name,
those wheely-bins add to my all-up weight
when orange overalls call at your gate.
Collection and disposal is our game.

If we do not arrive you'll phone and claim
the environmental officer's to blame
for failing to forewarn he'd changed the date.
The diet's never changed

with sacks of household waste, but I've one aim
to swallow just to satisfy my frame -
like Oliver, who asked for more, I wait
in hope that you will leave another plate
of your domestic scraps, but it's a shame
the diet's never changed.

R H M Vere

THE WAY

It grows dark in these woods for our family,
But hope before nightfall to find our way.
If we were lost in the clear light of day,
How shall we fare when we no longer see?
Yon tree has a familiar look - no doubt
Because we passed it several times before.
From wrong turns and stumblings of heretofore
May we learn at length and so find our way out.

So many times we thought the woods were past,
Only to find that it was just a clearing;
Beyond were woods much darker and more vast,
And now, because of greater fearing,
We come to lean upon our guide at last,
To hear His voice and know His touch so cheering.

V M Archer

TO BAGHDAD, BECAUSE . . . OF FREEDOM

Because tonight there are different sounds to fill in the encroaching
desert
Freedom hovers above silent words once fallen from faces inert
Of men and children waving from behind collapsing walls of conquest
At last this is the hour all forgotten captives will request

Freedom hovers above silent words once fallen from faces inert
For there is no space to measure this happiness thrown to unfathomable
test
At last this is the hour all forgotten captives will request.
No more fear where only the Khamsin wind will blow any remnant
doubt left.

For there is no space to measure this happiness thrown to unfathomable
test
Of men and children waving from behind collapsing walls of conquest
No more fear where only the Khamsin wind will blow any remnant
doubt left
Because tonight there are different sounds to fill in the encroaching
desert

Luisa Allan

PISCATOR REALITY

Blue shark
Silver ling
Arrow gar
Red herring

Silver ling
Freckled plaice
Red herring
Thorny ray

Freckled plaice
Glistening bass
Cold sole
Rainbow wrasse

Glistening bass
Arrow gar
Rainbow wrasse
Blue shark

In the net
Icy hold
On the quay
Market
Sold!

Roger Butts

UNTITLED

Willie was a little sod
Stuffed tomatoes down the bog
Workers at the sewage station
Thought a plague had hit the nation

Willie got his mother's pills
Chucked them in the farmers' fields
Though the cows were still receptive
Will had fed them contraceptive

Willie's an obnoxious child
Takes an interest in the wild
Fascinated by wet turds
Scattered All Bran for the birds

Mother tried to touch her toes
Wasn't wearing any clothes
Willie pushed the bedroom door
Laughed until his throat was sore.

Dorothy Blakeman

MADEMOISELLE KYRIELLE

You were the sunshine in her sky,
Now darkened as the days go by,
You left her with no sweet farewell,
Will you return to Kyrielle?

You never saw the tears she cried,
How would you know if she has died?
Lost in memories she does dwell,
Will you return to Kyrielle?

She hears your music piped on air,
Could it be you still hold some care,
For your lovely mademoiselle?
Will you return to Kyrielle?

So take up courage and step bold,
Come back to her now you are told,
For she to you has much to tell,
Will you return to Kyrielle?

A-ha! There on wind he blows sweet,
A chance with her again to meet.
'Marry me,' he rings the church bell.
He has returned to Kyrielle.

Carol Ann Darling

CAMPBELL'S BLUEBIRD

Bluebird! Bluebird!
As your engine purred,
Bluebird! Bluebird!
Hearts and minds stirred.

Bluebird! Bluebird!
Awed. Many held their breath,
Bluebird! Bluebird!
As you sped the watery breadth.

Bluebird! Bluebird!
Cruel fate on Coniston Water lake,
Bluebird! Bluebird!
Brought, your wake, within your wake.

Bluebird! Bluebird!
You inspired more than you knew;
Bluebird! Bluebird!
I pay tribute to you.

Donna June Clift

THE DRAMATICS

Our village boasts a dramatic society.
Their productions douce and 'safe' as propricty.
The same old offerings year after year -
Pawky wee 'one-actors' sure of a cheer.

Now Netta's the dame who says, 'I'm in charge.'
Where angels fear to tread, she'll barge.
Rebellious souls, from time to time
Have said, 'I've had it - I'm going to resign!'

The minister, young and new to the place,
Suggests, 'Let's try a change of pace.
This kailyard stuff's OK, but it palls,
How about Priestley's 'Inspector Calls'?

Brows are drawn, opinions muttered,
Then Netta stood up, looking grim as she uttered,
'We should avoid these highbrow shows,
And stick to what the audience knows.'

As for 'in-fights' and 'back-bites' at every meeting,
They've got politicians soundly beaten.
Different opinions and attitudes rage -
There's more 'dramatics' than on the stage.

The minister, poor soul, like a clerical Jack Horner,
Strategically leaves the scene - retires into the corner!

Margaret M Osoba

DREAMS

He lay on the veranda
Looking over the sea
Saw the bluebird
Sing in the tree.
The mountain seemed
So far away
He once had walked
That way
The sunlight faded
His toffee and cream
The sweet little cloud
Drowned his dreams.

Helen Owen

RONDELET

Where is that cat?
I think the dog has gone as well.
Where is that cat?
The two of them are much too fat.
They may be playing in the dell,
If weight be lost it's just as well.
Where is that cat?

E Marcia Higgins

SPRING

A hyacinth's heart-catching blue,
Crocuses of kingly hue,
Daffodils resounding hope,
The thrushes dawn-enchanted note.

A soft, bright sky, a budding tree,
Nest building in the shrubbery;
Ploughed land, swift silver surge of rain;
And warmth within the heart again.

E Osmond

ODE TO LOVE

Walking the world with you,
smiles for everyone . . .
under a patch of blue

Making time for a view
or just having fun . . .
walking the world with you

Sometimes rain, it's true
and we have to run . . .
under a patch of blue

Stars fall, wishes come true,
one by one . . .
walking the world with you

Nor shall death win through,
twin souls undone . . .
under a patch of blue

May Heaven guide true
for everyone . . .
walking the world with you
under a patch of blue

R N Taber

RESURRECTION

Our crucified Lord
Rose from his tomb that morning
And death was vanquished.

Roma Davies

HAMMY THE HAMSTER!

At half-past eight every night,
Out from the shadows comes a hairy sight.
Stretching and yawning, hair all over the place,
Don't look in the mirror, you look a disgrace.
With a sniff and a snuffle and a check - all is right,
He ambles stealthily along in dim light.
With paw on the edge, he climbs right upon,
His favourite toy, for his night-time song.
With a clickety-click, the whole house knows,
He's trying to make his head touch his toes!
For Hammy the hamster is on his wheel,
He goes on and on, becoming one with the reel.
'Hammy's out,' the children shout,
Highlight of the evening, without a doubt!

D Parry

THE EIGHTEENTH OF JUNE

In my garden on my late Grandmother's birthday
wafting to me, comes the scent of new-mown hay.
Honeysuckle, sweet williams, rose on the briar
and my philadelphus white with perfumed flower.

Today, I recall her garden long years ago
where all these flowers and others used to grow.
Her Madonna lilies and pinks were scented too
and lily of the valley in profusion grew.

She was born eighteenth of June, 1883
at Holtwood in Dorset in Framptons' family.
So, on her birthday, she is in my thoughts today
because . . . she was special in every way.

Valerie Ovais

FOREVER FRIENDS

It's forty years since we first met
The day in Junc I won't forget
The sea was calm, the sky so blue
A day made perfect meeting you
It only seems like yesterday
I asked you out that sunny day
My friend said, 'Frank, you must be mad
God help you when you meet her dad.'
Oh well, we met and he was great
Not like a dad, more like a mate
We've had some laughs along the way
And had our share of debts to pay
But all in all it ain't been bad
Although at times a little sad
But friends and family saw us through
And memories have helped us too
So if at times things don't look bright
Don't worry love, we'll be alright
In forty years we've done our best
So let's keep trying with the rest
And when it's time to add life up
Just order me another cup

Frank Osborne

THE RED KITE

Long had I waited for this summer day;
Now it was my time to go out and play.
I hurried across the familiar landscape
To a place that was perfect to make my escape.

'Twas a grassy knoll, bereft of trees
And there I felt a springy breeze.
Slowly and carefully, I knelt down,
Opening up my parcel of brown.

I took from it my kite of red,
Then through my hands, the string I fed.
I watched the kite take to the air
And soon my mind had joined it there.

We travelled across the azure sky;
Suddenly realised that I could fly.
I glanced below and on the ground,
Saw places I would ne'er have found.

As fields and meadows passed us by,
And white clouds scudded 'cross the sky,
And sunbeams danced on silver stream,
'Twas then I knew 'twas all a dream.

I needed to feel this freedom again,
Through mem'ries returned with such a great pain
Of dear friends, long gone, who used to play
With kites of red on a fine summer day.

Hazel Mills

FOREVER

Forever green, the field
In which I stand
Let my life be
As fertile as this land

Forever gold, the sun
Upon its trip
With rays of light
From which my mind may sip

Forever blue, the waters
Where I fish
And may I bathe in love
Oh, grant this wish

Forever white, the clouds
That float on high
From truth and justice
Never let me shy.

Kim Montia

SENSUALITY OVER INTELLECT

Suddenly realising the reason
Why things of beauty end, evaporate,
Of what lies behind the reason for change
When two become one then separate.

When in the process of becoming one,
Sensuality over intellect,
Moving towards this mode unconsciously,
The process of oneness did not suspect.

Once this state is attained, intellect rules,
Before it was purely a sixth sense,
When not controlling a situation,
Creative energy without pretence.

When achieving its goal, the ultimate,
Energy stops, intelligence now reigns,
Intellect is not the creative force,
Creativeness is in senses, not brains.

After, intellect picks up the chaos,
Having to analyse experience,
Justify, moralise, philosophise,
Psychoanalyse, using common sense.

But, in a very bad situation,
Pretends it is still the creative force
When it is only the worst impostor,
The outcome leads finally to divorce.

At the very heart, we want to prolong
Satisfaction of creativity,
Control it according to reason,
But there's no choice re sensuality.

Betty Mealand

FENLAND SUMMER

I often let my thoughts drift back,
To Fenland summers of my youth,
Where all earth was ocean-flat,
And wide horizons held the truth.

Beside the duckweed-covered dyke,
Where treeless acres reached the sky,
I flew a yellow paper kite,
While red-faced women cycled by.

I watched old Matt out on the land,
With leather reins, on iron seat,
His team, responding to his hand,
Cut furrows in the shaven wheat.

And seabirds filled the fields afar,
Like snowflakes on a winter's morn,
They chased the plough, and shone like stars,
Against the grey of coming storm.

I walked back home, before the rain,
Along the straight and dusty drove,
Then saw the farm, two miles away,
And watched the smoke from Maggie's stove.

She waved the tea-towel in her hand,
As if on board a ship at sea,
I hurried as the rain began,
While Maggie carved boiled ham for tea.

Fuzz Pendell

NOT JUST A DREAM

Not just a dream
One can travel far
With feelings supreme
Seeking their star

With thy feet on the ground
And the heavens above
Just look around
Everything befitting as a glove

Away with the harsh
Nothing be gained
It will never last
Just cause strain

With mind in order
Thou sail thro' each day
Without many a falter
With feelings in array

Oft one doth wonder
What be the future
And thou may ponder
One being not sure

Shadows fall across the sky
One can depend
As hearing distant birds cry
The unexpected may happen!

Josephine Foreman

To The Son I'll Never Know

Today I had a baby boy,
The greatest gift of all,
A gift of life, a wonder to behold,
You bring to me such joy,
To have and hold you,
A newborn baby, to love and cherish,
His tiny little hands and little feet,
I have waited a lifetime to meet,
To show him to the world,
I would like you all to greet
My bright, beautiful baby boy,
With soft down hair and lovely eyes,
A skin so tender and soft to touch,
I'm so very glad to know you,
I love your little face and your smile,
Always remember I love you,
I would gladly give my life for you.

C Forfar

FIRST TIME

She pulled him to her gentle breast,
And then to him laid this request.
'Though in this moment love will shine,
For always will your love be mine?'

The kiss was soft as was reply,
'I'll love thee love until I die.'
'Not just when lips and bodies twine,
For always will your love be mine?'

'Forever and a day, my sweetness,
You will make me feel completeness.'
'And when I'm far away you'll pine,
For always will your love be mine?'

'As long as you don't change t'wards me,
I'll keep the vows I made to thee.
Now I ask you my Clementine,
For always will your love be mine?'

She lifted him so their eyes met,
'Don't let me look back with regret,
You're mine, I'm yours, I'm yours, you're mine,
For always will your love be mine!'

Sid 'de' Knees

DEM BONES

Dem bones are not much use to me
Cos they just creak and crack
My friends can hear me coming
Is there something that I lack?

I go about my daily chores
And do the best I can
And find that if I sit too long
I'll need an oilcan.

I get up in the morning
Not knowing what to do
And I have to put my weight on them
When sitting on the loo.

Sometimes they cause me so much pain
I bare it all and yet
I have been to see the doctor
Now I think I'll see a vet.

But still I must rely on them
To help me stand up straight
Or else I'd slide around the floor
Like jelly on a plate.

B Smith

CAPTIVE HEART

Who will wrap my heart in golden chains,
Take away my heavy earthly pains?
Touch my lips with angel's kiss
Take me to eternal bliss.

Who will fill me with a heavenly fire,
Fuelled by passion and desire?
Take me to that other place,
Far beyond all sight and trace.

Keep me captive evermore
Floating inches from the floor.
Always on the precipice,
Ready for that sweetest kiss.

Hold me through the blackest night,
Take away my fears, make everything right.
Laugh with me, at me, share good and bad,
Salve my ego, don't let me be sad.

And when the lights are going dim,
And life is ebbing, and all looks grim,
Hold tight to all the dreams we've shared,
And prove that every day we cared.

So who will wrap my heart in those golden chains,
And take away my heavy earthly pains?
Touch my lips with angel's kiss,
And take me to eternal bliss . . . ?

Brian L Porter

COME ON YOU REDS

Thank you very much for giving me red hair,
didn't you realise that nobody likes it there?
They call me 'Ginger Nut' or the 'Weakest Link',
they say I look like Anne Robinson and try to make me wink.
I've even got red freckles all over my face,
and I have to wear a hat if I go out any place.
What is it people laugh at just for being a redhead?
It's no different from any other colour, what would they like me
to have instead?
Purple, green, blue or black or maybe baby pink?
No! It's not my fault, I must stop worrying what people think.
I suppose I should be thankful, it was meant to be this way,
I'll hold my head up high and proud, who cares what people say?

Nicola Pitchers

Passing Our Time Away

Life's too short to worry
What people say or do,
About the friendship that we have,
My neighbour dear and true.

They all may tittle-tattle
About the time we share
In company with each other,
But I don't really care.

We know it is platonic,
Our relationship is rare
And it makes our days less lonely
Now our partners are not there.

So we'll carry on our friendship
And not worry what they say
As we go out for our shopping
Just to pass our time away.

Kathleen South

UNEXPECTED VISITOR!

He should have been here yesterday,
And now the morning's come.
Still no sign, or word of mouth,
Because I am his mum.
I'm sure most things are right for him,
It's 'cause he likes to please.
Exactly like his ma you see,
He cuts himself in threes!

Lyn Sandford

FOREST PATH

As I walked through the forest
my eyes were focused on the floor.
I slipped and banged my head
as I had done many times before.
My head was grazed and throbbing
and not to say a little sore.
When I eventually came to a cottage
I banged upon its door.
Someone answered and said,
'What have you done to your head?'
By now the sun was setting,
sinking low and turning red.
I asked if they had a spare bed,
slept there and in the morning fled.
When I awoke, nobody was there,
for years they had been dead.
I have never found the cottage again,
though very often the forest path I do tread.

S Glover

KESTREL OF THE GLEN

Poised, motionless, eyes fixed on distant glen,
Each sign of life is spotted from your perch,
A lofty stump of frozen, sprawling birch,
Your patient hourly vigils start again;
Surveying frozen tracks on mountain height,
You see an aged crofter search for stock,
With trusty dog, he gathers up his flock,
All moving things are kept within your sight.

A creature spied, you wing your skyward flight,
Hovering high above with silent skill,
You dive at last, claws clutching at your kill,
Then wheel away until you're out of sight.
Aerodynamic beauty shows your power,
You're watching still throughout each daylight hour.

Norma Rudge

THOSE DANCING TREES

Those dancing trees swirling round and round
The rhythm's in my heart
Skimming the sky with rustic sound

Your gentle arms surround
Moving together from the start
Those dancing trees swirling round and round

In your nimble feet I'd found
Harmony floating like a lark
Skimming the sky with rustic sound

Twisting and turning as if bound
As one never to part
Those dancing trees swirling round and round

Skipping so lightly lest we pound
Wonderful journeys in our magical cart
Skimming the sky with rustic sound

Gliding and riding in the park
My graceful angel crowned
Those dancing trees swirling round and round
Skimming the sky with rustic sound

Adele C W Lane

THE CAT AND THE GOLDFISH

Our cat jumped on the sideboard,
And sat near the goldfish bowl,
As she watched the fish swim round and round,
She said to herself, 'I could swallow you whole.'

She pressed her nose up to the bowl,
And licked her lips in delight,
The poor fish panicked and tried to get out,
He got such a terrible fright.

Then pussy had a brainwave,
Dipped her paw in at the top,
She almost touched the water,
Before I shouted, 'Stop.'

But as she touched the water,
With her little furry paw,
The poor fish at the bottom thought,
I can't take anymore.

I had watched this whole performance
With my camera carefully poised,
To snap this vital moment,
And didn't make a noise.

He thought his life was over,
Till I lifted pussy down,
Then up he came and preened himself,
Joyfully swimming round and round.

Iris Covell

BLUEBELL WOOD

Like to find it again.
Taken there in my childhood.
Never again discover Bluebell Wood
Where speckled woods
Flit in dappled light.
Cream and down butterflies dance up and down,
Up to the tree heights.

Under the trees, Oxford blue bluebells
In every direction,
Down to fairy dell.
Sightseeing sight, cast a magic spell,
Some shade of pink, odd white.
Overwhelming smell of the upright,
Of wild Spanish hyacinths mixed.

With the English hyacinths, sprawling habits,
Hiding the holes of the inhabitants,
The fluffy rabbits.
Aloof in treetops,
Twiggy rookery nests,
In their black Sunday suits,
The rooks look their Sunday best.

Buzz of a batch of bluebottles,
Paint to point, by the stinging nettles,
Bluebells tucked under the bushes with bees bustling.
April, May magic.
It's tragic
When it comes to an end,
Which it tends to do.

B G Clarke

THIS LIFE

This humdrum world we live in
So commercialised today
Gone are the days when one carries cash
It's plastic all the way
'How are you paying?' the cashier asks
'Just put it on my card.'
But when you get (the big bill)
You wish you never had
And all the gadgets we possess
I suppose they do some good
But the world, it changes every day
But then we knew it would
It's so very, very easy just to lose your way
With pressure that's upon us
From people on the prey
Getting us to take out loans and lots of other kinds
Happy just to see you, but don't you get behind
So before you sign the dotted line
Just think before you do
Do we really need all of this
That people give to you?

N Carruthers

BOA CONSTRICTOR

His eyes are metallic gold
His skin the finest leather
And through the night he strolled
Slithering, sliding, a creature cajoles
Hunting prey in all kinds of weather
His eyes are metallic gold
Terrifying stalkers, snakes, controlled
Searching beneath dense heather
When through the night he strolled
Creeping floor this phantom patrolled
Armoured scales, limbless reptile cleaver
His eyes are metallic gold
A deadly serpent, mighty and bold
Worming his way, light as a feather
When through the night he strolled
Constricting with his powerful hold
Gaping jaws grab hold, tightly tether
His eyes are metallic gold
When through the night he strolled

Ann Hathaway

THE STORY OF BELINDA JANE

Belinda Jane was a pretty little girl
Whose hair was straight without a single curl
She dressed in trousers, never a dress
Plump Mama thought she looked such a mess
But this little girl loved to run and climb trees
She was more at home with the birds and the bees
But on this sad day she had such a fright
Her friends came to play with a big bright kite
So she laughingly took the long rope
And went running wildly over the slope
Puff went the wind and up she did sail
High over the hill and up the dale
Belinda Jane, Belinda Jane
Where are you going with your golden mane?
Arms and legs a cross in the sky
She somersaulted and tumbled into a sty
There she lay like a scarecrow of hay
Up she scrambled and made fast for home
'Mama, Mama, where is that dress and comb
I want to be a little girl
Who knits and sews and has ringlets and a curl.'

Frances Ann Hall

DRIVING TEST

You're going on your driving test
Your stomach's at your feet
You hope that all those people
Go home and clear the street

You've arrived at the test centre
Your examiner's on the scene
His calming words put you at ease
It's as calm as you have been

You read the chosen number plate
You read it with such ease
Now you're in the driving seat
'When you're ready please.'

You settle down, turn the key
And select the perfect gear
Gas goes down, clutch comes up
You wish you were not here.

You leave the centre silently
It looks a busy day
The traffic's now approaching
And you begin to pray.

Your nerves of steel are shattered
You've butterflies below
'Remember, there's a speed limit
Please do not drive too slow.'

The three point turn was easy
So was parking in a bay
Off you go with more to do
Hoping they all go this way.

The test, it was quite easy
And back you go at last
You pull into the centre
'You'll be pleased to know you've passed.'

You grin at your instructor
You're oh so full of pride
Shake hands, swap seats, relax
Sit back, enjoy the ride.

J L Preston

THE NIGHT IN SUMMER

The night is calm when we are at rest,
When we give only our best.
The majesty of beauty's storm
Without life or form,
That strikes a chord in our hearts.
From this beauty we will never part.
The glowing of eyes
Where beauty lies.
The burning of our limbs,
As the night gradually dims.

I T Hoggan

BLUEBOTTLE

Busy, bothersome, buzzing fly,
Syphoning up my cocoa,
I'm warning you. Prepare to die.
Your antics drive me loco.

You land upon my toast and cheese
With undercarriage mucky,
Thinking to live a life of ease.
Fly, you should be so lucky.

You settle on my wrist or arm,
Looking self-satisfied,
Thinking you will not suffer harm
From planned insecticide.

You stroll across my Dundee cake
Like Cortes crossing Darien.
Come on, get off, for Heaven's sake,
You filthy wee barbarian.

You slalom on my furrowed brow -
Perhaps you think it scenic?
Now. Now, you beast. Your moment's now -
Your feet are unhygenic.

They've wandered over nameless muck,
Middens of odd enzymes.
And yet - you always seem to duck
My copy of the Times,

Rolled up as tight as a mugger's cosh.
I swat. I flail. *Drop dead!*
Dead you are not. It seems, by gosh,
You've eyes all round your head.

You look at me with acute derision
And panoramic vistavision.

Norman Bissett

FUTURISTIC WINDOW CLEANER

Brr! It's cold! But I still have to work,
Because I'm freezing I just can't shirk.
Where's my bucket and leather?
I hate the wet scrim in this sort of weather,
And climbing the ladder is a slippery task,
Why can't I lie in the sun and simply just bask?
If I could invent a windowless house,
I could live underground like a small harmless mouse,
Or perhaps I could use my brain to think up
A portable heater to carry in a cup.
Best of all I need a backpack (jet-propelled of course),
Like a Pegasus to be a high-flying horse.
I'd fly up there from pane to pane,
Then drop to the ground without breakage or strain.
Ah! Me! I'm no spaceman and that's for sure.
I wish I could invent an aching back cure!

Evelyn Balmain

WINE

There's something to be said for wine,
It's something you cannot define,
When pressed to drink who could decline
Such wondrous products of the vine?
It's good for when you rest, recline,
It's great at parties, when you dine,
Or when with old friends you combine.
With each fresh glass, you feel divine,
It sends a tingle down your spine.
Your inhibitions soon untwine,
Your spirits soar, you're on cloud nine.
Each partner is your Valentine.

Next morning, you do not feel fine,
You hate the very thought of wine.
Your head is throbbing, you opine,
Your mouth now tastes of turpentine
And stagnant sewage from the Tyne.
You loathe that person, asinine,
Who made you try wines from the Rhine,
Mixed with non-vintage Argentine.
You're sorry for yourself and whine,
'Next time I'll drink beer from a stein.'
Contritely, you recall that line:
'The Lord says vengeance shall be mine!'

Jax Burgess